# PREFACE

This report provides a description and assessment of Internet-accessible databases relevant for social science research on terrorism. The body of this report details those websites that provide actual data, e.g., names of terrorist organizations and incidents of terrorist activity; several have search capabilities. These websites are maintained primarily by U.S. government agencies, non-U.S. research centers, and international organizations. An appendix to this report provides an extensive list of additional resources that provide commentary and analysis of terrorism events and trends. These resources are derived from the U.S. government, libraries, international agencies, government and private non-U.S. agencies and institutes, and academic-based domestic organizations.

No one definition of terrorism can be applied to all the databases referenced herein. As the National Institute for the Prevention of Terrorism states on its website: "There is no universally accepted definition of terrorism and even when people agree on a definition of terrorism, they sometimes disagree about whether or not the definition fits a particular incident." (<http://www.mipt.org/terrorismdefined.asp>)  In instances where a specific database has adopted a definition of terrorism, the report so notes.

This report indicates the focus of each database, including whether or not it is restricted to a particular region of the world, but it is not the role of the authors to present any bias that may be reflected in the selection of data.

## Table of Contents

**Name:** **U.S. STATE DEPARTMENT COUNTERTERRORISM OFFICE**

**Address:** <http://www.state.gov/s/ct>

**Definition of Terrorism:** In its report *Patterns of Global Terrorism 2002,* the U.S. State Department states: "No one definition of terrorism has gained universal acceptance. For the purposes of this report, we have chosen the definition in 22 USC 2656f (d): terrorism means premeditated, politically motivated violence against persons or property to intimidate or coerce a government, the civilian population, or any segment thereof, in furtherance of political or social objectives."

**Focus of Data:** International

**Database Contents:**

    (1) Counterterrorism Office - brief biography of counterrorism coordinator and statement of U.S. counterterrorism policy; link to White House *Progress Report on the Global War on Terrorism.* Link to database on Foreign Terrorist Organizations (fact sheet on statutory authority, designation method and criteria, and list of FTOs, current as of May 23, 2003).

    (2) Counterterrorism current events - summary of recent activity.

    (3) Diplomacy and the Global Coalition Against Terrorism - link to department publication *United Against Terrorism*, related information from the White House, and legislation. Section on Terrorists and Terrorism has link to FTO list and Terrorist Exclusion List (see Counterterrorism and Finance, below).

    (4) Patterns of Global Terrorism - link to full text of report *Patterns of Global Terrorism 2002*, released April 2003, and earlier annual reports (report gives overviews of terrorism by geographic region; appendices include background information on FTOs and other terrorist groups; chronology of significant terrorist incidents, 2002; summary of the U.S. military counterterrorism campaign in 2002). This page also has a link to archives, which includes FTO designations for 1997 and 1999.

    (5) International Programs - discussion of major initiatives with other U.S. agencies and foreign nations to improve preparation, deterrence, and response to terrorist attacks.

    (6) Counterterrorism Finance and Designation Unit - Attorney General's statement on terrorist financing, and links to press statements on recent (early 2003) designations of terrorist groups/organizations. Links to the following databases:

        • Foreign Terrorist Organizations, which "this Unit leads and coordinates with the U.S. Department of Treasury and the Department of Justice to designate."

        • Executive Order (EO) 13224 authorizes the U.S. government to

1

designate and block the assets of foreign individuals and entities that commit, or pose a significant risk of committing, acts of terrorism. There is a link to the text of this EO, and a fact sheet, with a further link to the Treasury Department Office of Foreign Assets Control list of persons/entities whose assets were blocked as of September 23, 2001, current as of October 24, 2003, and updated continually.

- Terrorist Exclusion List - fact sheet on statutory authority; designation criteria; and list of designees, current as of February 18, 2003.

(7) Homeland Security Unit - paragraph on relationship between Department of State and Office of Homeland Security; link to Secretary's statement on passage of Homeland Security Act.

(8) Countering Terrorism - links to EO13224, White House statements, Congressional activity against terrorism, and chronologies of September through December 2001 events, 1963-1999 treaties, and 1961-2001 incidents. Link to table of international terrorism conventions and text of UN, NATO, European Union, OAS and Caribbean Community resolutions/declarations.

(9) Related Sites - government and non-government

(10) Releases - text of remarks, reports, fact sheets, press releases

**Data Sources:** Primary government source.

**Database Access:** Full access from Internet Explorer and Netscape.

**Access charges:** Free.

**Limitations on Data Use:** "External links to other Internet sites should not be construed as an endorsement of the views contained therein."

**Tutorial Assistance:** None; access to all information is by simply arranged links, with full range of movement among database segments.

**Codebooks:** None.

**References Related to Using the Dataset:** None.

**Requirements for Using the Dataset:** None.

**Data Assessment:**

This website is a primary government source, and should be considered as an authoritative source for names of individuals and groups linked to terrorism. This information is provided in three separate lists: Designated Foreign Terrorist Organizations; Terrorist Exclusion List (used for immigration purposes); and list of

2

organizations and individuals linked to terrorism, whose assets have been blocked pursuant to Executive Order (EO) 13224. The background information provided with each list enables the user to understand the basis upon which those named have been included.

This website was initially confusing to the user because of multiple links to the abovementioned lists. Much has been done to consolidate the links, particularly regarding the list of persons and entities impacted by EO 13224, which can be found only on the Treasury Department Office of Foreign Assets Control website. However, the *Counterterrorism Finance and Designation Unit* page still has two references to the EO, which the user might think links to two different types of information, but in fact both link to the OFAC page, which includes a fact sheet and list of designees.

## Name: U.S. TREASURY DEPARTMENT OFFICE OF FOREIGN ASSETS CONTROL (EXECUTIVE OFFICE FOR TERRORIST FINANCING AND FINANCIAL CRIME)

**Address:** <http://www.treasury.gov/offices/eotffc/ofac/index.html>

**Definition of Terrorism**: None given.

**Focus of Data**: International

**Database Contents:**

(1) Specially Designated Nationals and Blocked Persons (list of individuals and entities with which U.S. persons are precluded from dealing; those named are either associated with international narcotics or terrorism or are owned or controlled by, or acting on behalf of, the governments of countries deemed hostile to U.S. foreign policy or national security objectives).
(2) Country-by-country summary of sanctions in force.
(3) Text of Executive Order 13224 and list of persons whose assets have been blocked pursuant to that Order.

**Database Sources:** Primary government source.

**Database Access:** Full access from Internet Explorer and Netscape.

**Access Charges:** Free.

**Limitations on Data Use:** None.

**Tutorial Assistance:** None; access to all information is by simply arranged links, with full range of movement among database segments.

**Codebooks:** None.

**References Related to Using the Dataset:** None.

**Requirements for Using the Dataset:** None.

**Data Assessment:**

Under a recent reorganization of the Treasury Department, the Office of Foreign Assets Control (OFAC) is no longer under a Division of Enforcement; it is now part of the newly created Executive Office for Terrorist Financing and Financial Crime. The OFAC website states the mission of the Office as follows: "Administers and enforces economic and trade sanctions based on U.S. foreign policy and national security goals against targeted foreign countries, terrorists, international narcotics traffickers, and those engaged in activities related to the proliferation of weapons of mass destruction." OFAC "acts under the Presidential wartime and national emergency powers, as well as authority granted by specific legislation, to impose controls on transactions and freeze foreign assets under US jurisdiction."

As noted above, Treasury's website has a link to the text of EO 13224 and to the list of persons affected by the sanctions it imposes; there is also a link to this information in several locations on the State Department website (see descriptions above).

The list of Specially Designated Nationals and Blocked Persons, which only appears on the OFAC website, is a 125-page detailed list of names, giving aliases and country affiliation, and where known, address, terrorist organization affiliation and passport number. The list is very current, and frequently updated.

**Name:** *THE NEW CONSOLIDATED LIST OF INDIVIDUALS AND ENTITIES BELONGING TO OR ASSOCIATED WITH THE TALIBAN AND AL-QAIDA ORGANISATION AS ESTABLISHED AND MAINTAINED BY THE 1267 COMMITTEE*

**Address:** <http://www.un.org/docs/sc/committees/1267/1267ListEng.htm>

**Definition of Terrorism**: None given.

**Focus of Data**: For Taliban associates, Afghanistan; for Al-Qaida associates, international.

4

**Database Contents:**
(1) List of individuals and entities belonging to or associated with the Taliban
(2) List of individuals and entities belonging to or associated with the Al-Qaida organization

**Data Sources:** Committee of the United Nations Security Council established pursuant to resolution 1267 to oversee the implementation of sanctions imposed by the Security Council on individuals and entities belonging or related to the Taliban, Usama bin Laden, and the Al-Qaida organization.

**Database Access:** Full access from Internet Explorer and Netscape.

**Access Charges:** Free

**Limitations on Data Use:** None.

**Tutorial Assistance:** None; access to all information is by simply arranged links, with full range of movement among database segments.

**Codebooks:** None.

**Original Purpose of the Study:** See "Data assessment," below.

**References Related to Using the Dataset:** None.

**Requirements for Using the Dataset:** None.

**Data Assessment:**

Security Council Resolution 1267 (1999), as amended by Security Council Resolutions 1333 (2000) and 1390 (2002), requires all Member States to impose sanctions against "Usama bin Laden, members of the Al-Qaida organization and the Taliban and other individuals, groups, undertakings and entities associated with them." These sanctions are:
> Freeze without delay any funds and other financial assets or economic resources
> Prevent the entry into or the transit through their territories
> Prevent the direct or indirect supply, sale, and transfer of all arms and military equipment.

These resolutions also establish a committee, consisting of all Members of the Security Council, mandated to seek from all Member States information regarding actions taken to implement the abovementioned sanctions. This committee is requested to "maintain an updated list, based on information provided by States and regional organizations, of the individuals and entities designated as being associated with Usama bin Laden, including those in the Al-Qaida organization." A September 2002 report of the Security Council

Monitoring Group tasked to assess the implementation of UN sanctions found that "the United Nations consolidated list continues to be one of the key instruments available to States in their efforts to implement the provisions requested of them in Resolution 1390 (2002)." The report states that this list "forms the basis for action by Governments" to freeze financial and economic assets; and impose a travel ban and arms embargo against those whose names appear on the list.

The list posted on the United Nations website is current as of September 23, 2003.


**Name:  CENTER FOR DEFENCE AND INTERNATIONAL SECURITY STUDIES TERRORISM PROGRAMME** (Lancaster University, Lancaster, England)

**Address:**  <http://www.cdiss.org/terror.htm>

**Definition of Terrorism**: None given.
**Focus of Data**: Political and international

**Database Contents:**

(1) Topical issues - "a regularly changing selection of comment and analysis based on issues currently under active study by members of CDISS."
(2) *The CDISS Database: Terrorist Incidents 1945 to 1998* - list of selected incidents that collectively "provide a snapshot of the wide-range of terrorist attacks and political violence experienced worldwide since World War II." Incidents are grouped by decade. For each incident, a brief description is provided giving place and number of casualties.

**Data Sources:**  Internal database. Research material of the Centre is supplemented by University Library collection of government publications, professional service journals and bulletins, and academic and research institute periodicals and monographs.

**Database Access:**  Full access from Internet Explorer and Netscape.

**Limitations on Data Use:**  None.

**Tutorial Assistance:**  None; access to database is available at clearly identified site.

**Codebooks:**  None.

**Original Purpose of the Study:**  "The CDISS Terrorism Programme aims to identify major trends in international political violence. An area of particular interest is the increasing linkage between terrorist groups in different parts of the world."

**References Related to Using the Dataset:** None.

**Requirements for Using the Dataset:** None.

**Data Assessment:**

The Centre for Defence and International Security Studies is an interdisciplinary research unit based in Lancaster University's Department of Politics and International Relations. It "exists to conduct research, raise awareness and stimulate debate on a wide range of defence and security issues relevant to both the United Kingdom and the International Community."

This database provides one - to two - sentence summaries of major terrorist incidents that occurred between 1945 and 1998. All regions of the world are covered. Information for the period 1999 forward is being compiled, but not yet available. As such, it is a valuable historical tool, since most incident databases concentrate on recent years. However, the information is provided only in chronological order, and the database has no search engine to enable the user to locate an incident if the exact date is not known.

**Name: INTERNATIONAL POLICY INSTITUTE FOR COUNTER-TERRORISM** (Herzliya, Israel)

**Address:** <http://www.ict.org.il>

**Definition of terrorism:** None given.

**Focus of Data:** Political; predominantly, but not exclusively, Middle East.

**Database Contents:**

   (1) News updates.
   (2) Articles and documents (over 240 articles, sorted by topic: Arab-Israeli conflict; counterterrorism; financing terrorism; international terrorism; non-conventional terrorism; state-sponsored terrorism; terrorism and criminal activity; and terrorist organizations) with full text link. Special coverage of Al-Qaida, the Kurdistan Worker's Party (PKK), and the Palestinian-Israeli peace process.
   (3) Databases. This section is divided as follows:
   - Terrorist Organization Profiles - List of over 50 names of organizations (worldwide), and affiliation; for each organization, there are links to more detailed information (history; ideology and strategy; terrorist activity; other articles and documents).
   - Terror Attack Database - Searchable database that includes selected

international terrorist and guerilla attacks for the years 1986 to the present. Search by organization name; method used; target type; location; date; and number of casualties.

- Arab-Israeli Conflict - Analysis of fatalities "on both sides of the current Palestinian/Israeli conflict." Searchable database of incidents and casualties that can be searched by type of incident; terrorist organization involved; method used; site targeted; location; and date.

(4) Counter-terrorism - Articles, documents, and updates on international activity, terrorism and law, and Israeli activity.

**Data Sources:** Internal database, as well as U.S. State Department *Patterns of Global Terrorism;* and Institute for Conflict Management (see *South Asia Terrorism Portal*).

**Database Access:** Full access from Internet Explorer and Netscape.

**Access Charges:** None.

**Limitation on Data Use:** None.

**Tutorial Assistance:** None; access to all information is by simply arranged links, with full range of movement among database segments.

**Original Purpose of the Study:** "ICT is a research institute and think tank dedicated to developing innovative public policy solutions to international terrorism."

**References Related to Using the Dataset:** None.

**Requirements for Using the Dataset:** None.

**Data Assessment:**

This website, based in Israel, has the heaviest concentration of information on the Palestinian-Israeli conflict. The section on "Counter-terrorism" includes a subsection for "Israeli counter-terrorist activity" but none for any Arab country. This website is unique for its coverage of this region. No other website available to U.S. users appears to be dedicated to the issues and terrorist organizations involved in the Middle East conflict.

The information provided on the 50+ terrorist organizations profiled is very detailed and is international in scope. The database of international terrorist and guerilla attacks "is not exhaustive, but is updated on a monthly basis."

**Name:** SOUTH ASIA TERRORISM PORTAL

**Address:** <http://www.satp.org>

**Definition of Terrorism**: None given.

**Focus of Data**: Political and religious, South Asia.

**Database Contents:**

For Bangladesh, Bhutan, India, Nepal, Pakistan, Sri Lanka, and Select States of India - Mizoram, Assam, Jammu and Kashmir, Manipur, Punjab, and Tripura - the following subsections can be accessed:

(1) Assessment - Evaluation of political climate and terrorist activity
(2) Backgrounder - Sources of current conflict
(3) Bibliography
(4) Data Sheets - Fatalities, attacks and incidents of violence
(5) Documents - Acts and Ordinances; political addresses and statements
(6) Timelines - Arrests, incidents, and government statements; by day and month for current years, by year for historic information
(7) Terrorist Groups - Overview of major groups, or list; both with links to more detailed information.

**Data Sources:** Internal research; some background reports "constructed from media reports."

**Access Charges:** Free, with offer to subscribe to *South Asia Intelligence Review.*

**Limitations on Data Use:** None.

**Tutorial Assistance:** None; access to all information is by simply arranged links, with full range of movement among database segments.

**Codebooks:** None.

**Original Purpose of the Study:** See "Data Assessment" below.

**References Related to Using the Dataset:** None.

**Requirements for Using the Dataset:** None.

**Data Assessment:**

This website is managed by the Institute for Conflict Management in New Delhi, India. The Institute was established in 1997 as a non-profit society "committed to the continuous evaluation and resolution of problems of internal security in South Asia." Its research projects cover a wide spectrum of topics.

The information provided by this site, including the latest news for those countries covered, is frequently updated. It appears to be the only website on terrorism that is solely dedicated to this region.

The format for the "Terrorist Groups" section varies. For some countries, like Pakistan, the database includes an overview with links, for each group named, to a lengthy review of the group's ideology, leadership strategies, activities, and terrorist incidents. For others, like Sri Lanka, a list of groups is given, with links to further information on some. The site has no "terrorist group" section for Bhutan, but both the "assessment" and "backgrounder" sections have links to discussions of individual groups.

### Name:  CENTER FOR DEFENSE INFORMATION TERRORISM PROJECT

**Address:**  <http://www.cdi.org/terrorism>

**Definition of Terrorism**:  Section on "Explaining Terrorism" addresses the difficulties involved in defining terrorism.

**Focus of Data**: International.

**Database Contents:**

(1) *Terrorist Networks* section highlights a geographic cross-section of individual terrorist organizations. Each group includes a general discussion and history, and, in brief, the group's leader, base, size, cause, funding, and major attacks. This section also provides the link to the website's main database: *CDI FACT SHEET*: *Current List of Foreign Terrorist Organizations and other Terrorist Organizations (as designated by the U.S. State Department)*. For each organization listed, a link is provided to the complete series of in-depth articles prepared by CDI on each of these groups. The list is followed by a short list of other primary sources that also provide the names of terrorists and terrorist organizations.

(2) *What's New* and *Responding to Terrorism* sections provide links to in-depth analysis of issues related to the war on terrorism, homeland security, and chemical and biological weapons.

(3) *Explaining Terrorism* section, started in July 2003, will present a series of papers examining the various aspects of terrorism. Currently on the website: paper

entitled *Terrorism: The Problems of Definition.*

**Data Sources:** U.S. State Department.

**Database Access:** Full access from Internet Explorer and Netscape.

**Access Charges:** None.

**Limitation on Data Use:** None.

**Tutorial Assistance:** None; access to all information is by simply arranged links, with full range of movement among database segments.

**Codebooks:** None.

**Original Purpose of the Study:** "CDI's Terrorism Project is designed to provide insights, in-depth analysis and facts on the military, security and foreign policy challenges as the United States, and the world, faces terrorism. The project will look at all aspects of fighting terrorism, from near-term issues of response and defense, to long-term questions about how the United States should shape its future international security strategy."

**References Related to Using the Dataset:** None.

**Requirements for Using the Dataset:** None.

**Data Assessment:**

The CDI's list of Foreign Terrorist Organizations (FTOs) is drawn from the State Department list, and begins with a brief but helpful statement on its history and purpose. Although the list itself can be accessed from the State Department Counterterrorism Office web page, CDI's list is sometimes more current than State's. In addition, each organization named on the list provides a link to a full profile of the group, including its history, activities, and leadership. CDI also provides the names of other lists of terrorists and terrorist organizations, including the United Nations list of Taliban and Al-Q'aida members/associates, which is omitted from most websites' "additional resources" lists (for more detail on this list, see separate entry).

**Name:** FEDERATION OF AMERICAN SCIENTISTS INTELLIGENCE RESOURCE PROGRAM LIST OF *LIBERATION MOVEMENTS, TERRORIST ORGANIZATIONS, SUBSTANCE CARTELS, AND OTHER PARA-STATE ENTITIES*

**Address:** <http://www.fas.org/irp/world/para/index.html>

**Definition of Terrorism:** Scope note states: "Some para-states engage in terrorism, which is defined by the United States government in Title 22 of the United States Code, Section 2656f(d) as premeditated, politically motivated violence perpetrated against noncombatant targets by subnational groups or clandestine agents, usually intended to influence an audience. For purposes of this definition, the term "noncombatant" is interpreted to include, in addition to civilians, military personnel who at the time of the incident are unarmed and/or not on duty. Acts of terrorism also include attacks on military installations or on armed military personnel when a state of military hostilities does not exist at the site, such as bombings against US bases in Europe, Saudi Arabia, or elsewhere."

**Focus of Data:** International.

**Database Contents:** List of over 350 para-state entities. For the majority of names, the database provides a link to a lengthy description of the group and its activities. Following that text, the database provides a list of "sources and resources," which in many instances includes reports prepared by the U.S. State Department.

**Data Sources:** Lengthy bibliography follows the list; the bibliography includes U.S. State Department reports and lists, and compilations compiled by private and non-U.S. sources.

**Limitations on Data Use:** None.

**Tutorial Assistance:** None; access to all information is by simply arranged links, with full range of movement among database segments.

**Codebooks:** None.

**Original Purpose of Study:** See "Data Assessment" below.

**References Related to Using the Dataset:** None.

**Requirements for Using the Dataset:** None.

**Data Assessment:**

The list of para-state entities links to a scope note that defines para-states as entities that "through various forms of direct action contest the legitimate monopoly states have on the use of violence within a specified geographical territory." It states that the scope of this list is "both current and retrospective, including both currently active and long defunct entities." The scope "generally follows that of the mandate of the U.S. National Security Council Special Assistant to the President for Transnational Threats, which addresses threats to U.S. security such as terrorism, cyber warfare and computer security, covert employment of weapons of mass destruction, narcotics trafficking, and international organized crime."

FAS emphasizes that "this directory of para-states is not a list of terrorist organizations, and is not constructed to supplement or complement the list of terrorist organizations of the US Department of State." The guide intentionally casts a wide net, and "includes both the nasty and the nice."

The list is valuable if used with the caveats provided above, especially the understanding that it is not meant to be a list of terrorist organizations. In most cases, the user is able to ascertain the source of the information provided, and can exercise judgment as to its merit.


### Name: **OKLAHOMA CITY NATIONAL MEMORIAL INSTITUTE FOR THE PREVENTION OF TERRORISM (MIPT)**

**Address:** <http://db.mipt.org/rand_68_97.cfm> (RAND Terrorism Chronology 1968-1997); <http://db.org/mipt_rand.cfm> (RAND-MIPT Terrorism Incident DB 1998-Present)

**Definition of Terrorism**: Applies definition set forth in statute:
> The term "terrorism" means premeditated, politically motivated violence perpetrated against non-combatanti targets by sub-nationalii groups or clandestine agentsiii, usually intended to influence an audience.
> The term "international terrorism" means terrorism involving citizens or the territory of more than one country.
> The term "terrorist group" means any group practicing, or that has significant subgroups that practice, international terrorism.

22 U.S.C. § 2656f(d)

i The U.S. Government has interpreted "noncombatant" to include, in addition to civilians, military personnel who at the time of the incident are unarmed or not on duty. Similarly, the U.S. Government considers attacks on military installations or on armed military personnel when a state of military hostilities does not exist at the site to be terrorist attacks.
ii In this context, sub-national means a grouping not recognized as a nation-state. This includes groups like the Provisional Wing of the Irish Republican Army, HAMAS (Islamic Resistance Movement) or Kahane Chai.

iii An example would be the attacks on dissidents carried out by secret agents of the Iranian government

**Focus of Data**: Pre-1998, international; 1998 to present, domestic and international.

**Database Contents:** Two databases compiled by the RAND corporation can be accessed through the MIPT website.

## RAND Terrorism Chronology (1968-1997)

(1) Reports generated from database of terrorist incidents, which can be searched by tactic, region of the world, or target, with input of specific time frame.

(2) Charts of incidents trends; incidents by tactic; incidents by target; incidents by region; death trends and comparison between 1968 and 1997 (for the U.S., U.K. and world total); and comparison of injuries and deaths between 1968 and 1997.

(3) Searchable database providing graphical summary of the incidents, injuries, and fatalities that occurred in either a selected region or country, or by a specified tactic or target, within a specified time frame.

(4) Searchable database to "find detailed information about terrorist incidents between 1968 and 1997 according to the selected perpetrator, target, tactic and geographical location with a time frame."

(5) Searchable database of incidents using key word.

## RAND-MIPT Terrorism Incident DB (1998-Present)

(1) Searchable database generating the following reports, with user providing specific time frame:
   - Death, injury, and incident counts, in each world region
   - International, domestic, and total incident count, in each world region
   - Number of incidents according to the type of weapon used, in each world region
   - Number of attacks conducted by the FARC (Revolutionary Armed Forces of Colombia), Hamas, ETA (Basque Fatherland and Freedom), LTTE (Liberation Tigers Tamil Eelam), and ASG (Abu Sayyaf Group) against specific targets.

(2) Searchable database of statistical summaries of incidents, arranged by name of terrorist organization, region, country, target, weapon, casualty, attacks claimed by perpetrators, and attacks classified as international or domestic incidents, all within a selected time frame.

(3) Searchable database allowing researchers to "Find detailed information about incidents [that] occurred between 1998 and present according to the selected terrorist organization, target, weapon, and geographical location with a time frame."

(4) Searchable database of incidents using key word.

**Data Sources:** The MIPT Database System was created by a partnership of the MIPT and the University of Oklahoma. The two databases covered in this report are described as MIPT sponsored, but were compiled by the RAND Corporation. "All information was taken from open source materials, such as newspapers, and every effort was made to verify the accuracy of the information found in the reports."

**Database Access:**  Full access from Internet Explorer and Netscape.

**Access Charges:**  Free.

**Limitations on Data Use:**  None.

**Tutorial Assistance:**  None; access to all information is by simply arranged links, with full range of movement among database segments.

**Codebooks:**  None.

**Original Purpose of the Study:**  MIPT was "created to collect information on all types of terrorism, including explosives, CBRN (Chemical, Biological, Radiological and Nuclear), agricultural and cyberterrorism." MIPT's goal is to make centralized information on terrorism public, "so that it might help policymakers, academics and local responders to better understand terrorism." The MIPT database serves to monitor all terrorism incidents worldwide, both domestic and international.

**References Related to Using the Dataset:**  None.

**Requirements for Using the Dataset:**  None.

**Data Assessment:**

The terrorist incident information contained in this database, which dates back to 1968, is easy to access and very detailed. In the section covering 1968 to 1997, the user can search the database of incidents by (a) tactic, (b) region of the world, or (c) target. A table is then generated giving, for (a), the type of tactic, for (b), the country, and for (c), the type of target, and the number of incidents for each. A click on the number of incidents links to a detailed report on each incident (the name and nationality of the perpetrator, where known; and the date and full description of the incident).

In the database covering 1998 to the present, the user can access tables in the same manner as described above, but the incident information is arranged by country, type of weapon used, and those attributed to five specific terrorist groups. (Note that if search option 3 in "database contents" above is selected, the user can search for incidents by any of a list of dozens of terrorist groups.) As in the database of the earlier time period, a click on the number of incidents links to a full report of each incident, including the published source of the information.

The 1998-Present database (accessed in October 2003) contains data updated on March 12, 2003. The tabulations and descriptions of incidents for each category cover different time periods: for incidents arranged by region, from 12/26/97 to 3/08/03; for incidents arranged by type of weapon, from 12/26/97 to 3/8/03; and for incidents arranged by the five terrorist groups, from 1/3/98 to 3/6/03.

A third database, the *MIPT Indictment Database*, is under development jointly by the University of Alabama at Birmingham and the University of Oklahoma. It will "record terrorist cases that have taken place in the U.S. since 1978."

Overall, the two databases described herein represent a very comprehensive and valuable resource of information on incidents of terrorism in the United States and abroad.

# APPENDIX

## TERRORISM DATABASES AND RESOURCES FOR SOCIAL SCIENTISTS

### UNITED STATES GOVERNMENT AGENCIES

CIA (www.cia.gov/terrorism/index.html
<http://www.cia.gov/terrorism/index.html>) - *War on Terrorism* page has links to
statements, testimony, and reports.
Defense Department (www.defendamerica.mil <http://www.defendamerica.mil>)
- General news.
FBI (www.fbi.gov/terrorinfo/terrorism.htm
<http://www.fbi.gov/terrorinfo/terrorism.htm>) - "Most Wanted" list; general
news.
FEMA (www.fema.gov/hazards/terrorism
<http://www.fema.gov/hazards/terrorism>) - Background; fact sheet.
General Accounting Office (www.gao.gov <http://www.gao.gov>) - *Special
Collections -Terrorism* lists dozens of publications, dating back to 1980.
Navy Department Library (www.history.navy.mil/library/guides/terrorism.htm
<http://www.history.navy.mil/library/guides/terrorism.htm>) - *Terrorism: A Navy
Department Library Research Guide* includes links to other resources,
bibliographies, and chronologies.
Naval Postgraduate School (<http://library.nps.mil/home/terrorism.htm>) Dudley
Knox Library *Terrorism* page includes bibliographies and directives; links to
reports, documents, fact sheets, other resources.
State Department Counterterrorism Office (www.state.gov/s/ct
<http://www.state.gov/s/ct>) - see full report.
State Department Office of International Information Programs
(<http://usinfo.state.gov/topical/pol/terror>) - *Response to Terrorism* page
provides summaries of, with link to full text of, most recent White House and
State Department briefings, letters, and statements, with link to earlier documents;
links to key documents, issue analysis, and other resources.
Treasury Department Office of Foreign Assets Control (Executive Office for
Terrorist Financing and Financial Crime)
(www.treasury.gov/offices/eotffc/ofac/index.html
<http://www.treasury.gov/offices/eotffc/ofac/index.html>)  - see full report.

### U.S. LIBRARIES

Library of Congress (Portals to the World - Selected Internet Resources:
Terrorism) (www.loc.gov/rr/international/hispanic/terrorism/terrorism.html

<http://www.loc.gov/rr/international/hispanic/terrorism/terrorism.html>) - links to online sources on bioterrorism; U.S., U.K., and international law; terrorism in specific countries; and specific terrorists and Al Qaida.

Library of Congress (Guide to Law Online: Terrorism Law) (www.loc.gov/law/guide <http://www.loc.gov/law/guide>) - links to sites of executive, judicial, and legislative branches of government; international organizations; legal guides; general and media resources.

Joyner Library, East Carolina University (www.lib.ecu.edu/govdoc/terrorism.html <http://www.lib.ecu.edu/govdoc/terrorism.html>) - *Attack on America* page provides links to research and background sources on Osama bin Laden and al-Qa'ida, as well as general, government, and research sources on terrorism generally.

University of Michigan Documents Center (www.lib.umich.edu/gov/docs/usterror.html <http://www.lib.umich.edu/gov/docs/usterror.html>) - *America's War Against Terrorism* page provides links to very extensive list of resources on September 11 attack and counter-terrorism.

University of Buffalo Libraries (<http://ublib.buffalo.edu/libraries/units/lml/govdocsubj/terrorism.html>) - news accounts of World Trade Center; background on domestic and international terrorism.


## INTERNATIONAL AGENCIES

Council of Europe (www.coe.int/T/E/communication_and_Research/Press/Theme_files/Terrorism <http://www.coe.int/T/E/communication_and_Research/Press/Theme_files/Terrorism>) - documents on combating terrorism, conference activities and conventions, links to additional resources.

European Union (<http://europa.eu.int/news/110901>) - updates on actions taken by the EU in response to the September 11 attacks.

Interpol (www.interpol.int/Public/Terrorism/default.asp <http://www.interpol.int/Public/Terrorism/default.asp>) - links to press releases and fact sheets on terrorist attacks; resolutions on terrorism.

NATO (www.nato.int/terrorism/index.htm <http://www.nato.int/terrorism/index.htm>) - press releases, statements,speeches by Secretary General.

United Nations Office on Drugs and Crime (www.unodc.org/unodc/en/terrorism.html <http://www.unodc.org/unodc/en/terrorism.html>) - "Global Programme against Terrorism" page includes link to full text of UN's 12 universal conventions and protocols on terrorism.

United Nations (Dag Hammarskjold Library Resource Page)

(www.un.org/depts/dhl/resources/terrorism
<http://www.un.org/Depts/dhl/resources/terrorism>) - includes legal agreements and UN actions against terrorism, and other conventions.
(www.un.org/depts/dhl/resources/terrorism/elinks.htm
<http://www.un.org/depts/dhl/resources/terrorism/elinks.htm>) - links to other websites, international documents, and chronologies of incidents and attacks.
United Nations Security Council
(www.un.org/docs/sc/committees/1267/1050E02.pdf
<http://www.un.org/docs/sc/committees/1267/1050E02.pdf>) - second report of Monitoring Group on implementation of sanctions provides extensive information regarding al-Qa'idah activities, particularly terrorist-related financial transactions.
United Nations list of Taliban and Al-Qaida members
(www.un.org/docs/sc/committees/1267/1267ListEng.htm
<http://www.un.org/docs/sc/committees/1267/1267ListEng.htm>) - see full report.

## NON-U.S. SOURCES (GOVERNMENT AND PRIVATE)

Centre for Defence and International Security Studies - Lancaster, England
(www.cdiss.org/terror.htm <http://www.cdiss.org/terror.htm>) - see full report.
Centre for the Study of Terrorism and Political Violence - University of St. Andrews, Scotland (www.st-andrews.ac.uk/~www_sem/IR/research/cstpv/research.html <http://www.st-andrews.ac.uk/~www_sem/IR/research/cstpv/research.html>) - describes International and Domestic Database Project, with contact information "for academic, media and general inquiries."
International Policy Institute for Counter-Terrorism - Herzliya, Israel
(www.ict.org.il <http://www.ict.org.il>) - see full report.
National Security Australia (Attorney General's Department)
(www.nationalsecurity.ag.gov.au <http://www.nationalsecurity.ag.gov.au>) - provides "single access point for national security information from the Australian Government."
Parliament of Australia - Department of the Parliamentary Library
(www.aph.gov.au/library/intguide/fad.terror.htm
<http://www.aph.gov.au/library/intguide/fad.terror.htm>) - Library research papers on terrorism and counter-terrorism; links to other sites.
South Asia Terrorism Portal (www.satp.org <http://www.satp.org>) - see full report.
University of Adelaide, Australia - Terrorism: A Guide to Library Resources for Anthropology (www.library.adelaide.edu/au/guide/soc/anthro/subj/terror.html
<http://www.library.adelaide.edu/au/guide/soc/anthro/subj/terror.html>) - references to encyclopedias, handbooks and directories.

**OTHER**

Anti-Defamation League (www.adl.org/main_terrorism.asp <http://www.adl.org/main_terrorism.asp>) - reports on terrorist activities and groups; emphasis on Middle East.

Anser Institute for Homeland Security (www.homelandsecurity.org <http://www.homelandsecurity.org>) - includes link to current and past issues of monthly "Homeland Security Newsletter."

Brookings Institution Foreign Policy Studies (www.brookings.edu/dybdocroot/terrorism <http://www.brookings.edu/dybdocroot/terrorism>) - provides commentary and analysis; links to other resources. www.brookings.edu/dybdocroot/fp/projects/homeland/homeland.htm <http://www.brookings.edu/dybdocroot/fp/projects/homeland/homeland.htm> provides links to chapters of Brookings' *Assessing the Department of Homeland Security*; links to other resources.

Center for Defense Information (www.cdi.org/terrorism <http://www.cdi.org/terrorism>) - see full report.

Emergency Response and Research Institute (ERRI) Counter-Terrorism Archive (www.emergency.com/cntrterr.htm <http://www.emergency.com/cntrterr.htm>) - news reports and links to articles, 1989 to present.

Federation of American Scientists (www.fas.org/terrorism/index.html <http://www.fas.org/terrorism/index.html>) - *America's War on Terrorism* page provides information and analysis on counter-terrorism, information security, and weapons of mass destruction. Intelligence Resource Program (www.fas.org.irp <http://www.fas.org.irp>) has section on Terrorism (background and threat assessments) that provides dozens of links to reports, documents, fact sheets, and government sources. Links to resource materials for the Taleban are provided at www.fas.org/irp/world/para/taleban.htm <http://www.fas.org/irp/world/para/taleban.htm>. See full report for description of directory of para-state entities. (www.fas.org/irp/world/para/index.html <http://www.fas.org/irp/world/para/index.html>)

FindLaw (<http://news.findlaw.com/legalnews/us/terrorism>) *Special Coverage: War on Terrorism* has subsections for news articles, commentary, court cases, documents, and laws. Documents section includes an extensive list of documents specific to the September 11 terrorist attacks; and under subtopic "Terrorism" (<http://news.findlaw.com/legalnews/us/terrorism/documents/terr.html>) there are dozens of links to reports of U.S. government agencies, the Congressional Research Service, academic institutions, and think tanks.

George Washington University - The National Security Archive (www.gwu.edu/~nsarciv <http://www.gwu.edu/~nsarciv>) - includes text of 6-volume work, *The September 11 Source Books* (Volume I - *Terrorism and U.S. Policy*).

Jurist (<http://jurist.law.pitt.edu/terrorism/terrorism.htm>) - *Terrorism Law and*

*Policy* subsection *Terrorism and Terrorists* includes links to government advisories and reports on terrorist groups and threat assessments.

Oklahoma City National Memorial Institute for the Prevention of Terrorism (www.mipt.org <http://www.mipt.org>) - links to subsection *Terrorism Incidents and Significant Dates*, which is a searchable database.

> *Rand Terrorism Chronology* (<http://db.mipt.org/rand_68_97.cfm>) - see full report.
>
> *Rand - MIPT Terrorism Incident DB* (<http://db.mipt.org/mipt_rand.cfm>) - see full report.

Monterey Institute of International Studies, Center for Nonproliferation Studies - CNS Subjects: Terrorism (<http://cns.miis.edu/research/terror.htm>) - links to articles and testimony on agroterrorism, terrorist group profiles, U.S. response to terrorism, and weapons of mass destruction. The Chemical and Biological Weapons Nonproliferation Program at CNS maintains a terrorism database, available on a subscription basis. CNS Subjects: Chemical and Biological Weapons (<http://cns.miis.edu/research/CBW>) - links to resources on the Americas, Middle East/Africa, Newly Independent States, and East Asia.

PolitInfo (www.politinfo.com/issues/Terrorism/terrorism.html <http://www.politinfo.com/issues/Terrorism/terrorism.html>) - links to general resources, think tanks and research centers, publications.

RAND Institution *Research Area: Terrorism* (www.rand.org/terrorism_area <http://www.rand.org/terrorism_area>) - highlights of recent work and ongoing research; news and commentary. Similar coverage for *National Security* (www.rand.org/natsec_area <http://www.rand.org/natsec_area>). National Security research website (www.rand.org/nsrd <http://www.rand.org/nsrd>) has link to page on Gilmore Commission (Advisory Panel to Assess Domestic Response Capabilities for Terrorism Involving Weapons of Mass Destruction), including text of four annual reports.

Henry L. Stimson Center (www.stimson.org <http://www.stimson.org>) - research on reducing the threat of weapons of mass destruction; building regional security; strengthening institutions of international peace; and linking trade, technology, and security.

Terrorism Research Center (www.terrorism.com/index.shtml <http://www.terrorism.com/index.shtml>) - analysis, essays, profiles of counter-terrorism groups and terrorist organizations, descriptions of terrorist attacks, and "Terrorism Bookshelf"(extensive bibliography, with summaries, of works on terrorism and homeland security).

www.ingramcontent.com/pod-product-compliance
Lightning Source LLC
Chambersburg PA
CBHW080406290526
45790CB00009BA/3722